Backyard Parables

Discovering Wisdom Close to Home

Walt Lichtenberger

Copyright © 2020 Walt Lichtenberger

All rights reserved.

Cover design by Casey Fuerst, Tic Tac Toe Marketing.

Cover Image by Mark Lichtenberger.

All scripture quotations are from the New Revised Standard Version, Bible, copyright 1989, Division of Christians Education of the National Council of the Churches of Christ in the United States of America. Used by permission. All rights reserved.

978-1-7345607-0-1

DEDICATION

To the loving memories of a storyteller and a gardener,

John Weite and Judi O'Connor

CONTENTS

CHAPTER FOUR

CHAPTER FIVE

CHAPTER SIX

CONCLUSION

PREFACE

In my blogs and devotional series, I often write about faraway travels. I like to share insights from visiting national parks and taking coastal drives. My imagination soars when I think about ancient ruins left in remote canyons. The context for this devotional book is a lot closer to home; it takes place in my backyard.

Some backyards are extravagant. I have been in yards with waterfalls and koi ponds. I have marveled with a hint of jealousy at backyard train layouts with miniature trees and tunnels. Spectacular and stunning. I have witnessed that considerable investments of time and money can produce settings that rival parks and botanical spaces. These are places that generate a feeling of "wow!"

My backyard is not a showplace and will never make the cover of a garden magazine. There is nothing particularly complicated or technical about it. The only moving parts that it contains are the creatures that come to visit. There is lawn, a small vegetable garden, beautiful flowers, a birdbath, a woodpile, compost bin, and perennial shrubs that line the border.

My backyard is an ordinary place where life happens and blooms. Sitting in a comfortable deck chair, drinking my morning coffee, I like to watch the sunrise through the trees to the east. I breathe deeply—sometimes even in prayer—as I sit and listen to the unsolicited but always appreciated chorus of songbirds.

Don't get me wrong; my backyard is not perfect. There you will find mud, weeds, and dog poop. As refreshing a space as it is, there are no pretensions. Its beauty takes work and tending. There are times when the other spheres of life demand attention and pull with a gravity that is inescapable. When that happens, the backyard gets wild and unruly.

Even if you have a landscaper or lawn service, your backyard is a place where you are likely to put on a pair of work gloves and get your hands dirty. Yards require a fair amount of work and care. There are tasks of planting and pruning to be done. Some greenery needs to be cut back while you allow other fauna free range. It is ironic that without care and hard work, backyards are probably not going to be a place of relaxation and sanctuary. Unattended backyards are usually avoided and are not a place where you gather and share life with friends.

From the second creation story in Genesis (2:4b–25), God beckons humanity to tend and care for the garden so that it might grow and flourish. Similarly, we are invited each day to attend to our spiritual gardens—nurture, water, prune, seed. These are spiritual activities that require thought, effort, and intention. At times, things will get unruly. In these moments, we need to stop, breathe, and refocus. Prayer, meditation, and Word/Sacrament-centered worship help to get us back on track and our spiritual backyards back in shape.

When Jesus preached and taught about God's Kingdom, he said that it was nearby. Jesus used parables—small teaching illustrations—to proclaim that the Kingdom of Heaven is close to where we live our lives. God's mysteries can be found and explored in common spaces that are literally in our backyard.

Each day offers us an opportunity. In the ordinary places of our lives, God is present and invites us to engage in spiritual living to grow as God's children and to love our neighbor. We don't need to travel to exotic and remote places to access God's wisdom. Simple experiences and nearby objects can teach us about the wonders of God's Kingdom. We need to look no further than our backyard to find a place of nurture, challenge, and growth.

I dedicate this book to the loving memory of two very special people who come immediately to mind when I think of backyards and wisdom. Though both have died, they live in my heart and I count my memories of their lives as enduring blessings.

The first is my grandfather, John Weite. As a teenager, I spent many afternoons sitting with him in my backyard. Grandpa was a master storyteller and shared countless tales with me about his life. During World War II, he served as a sergeant in the 166th bomb disposal unit. More than once, he ignited my imagination with his narratives. He remains an inspiration.

The second person is my mother-in-law, Judi O'Connor. She was the first person of the O'Connor family who I met in Utica, New York before starting my pastoral internship. Kindness and compassion were part of the driving values of her life. Granny O. (as her grandkids affectionately called her) was a hard worker who was filled with determination. Her garden was filled with interesting plants – dill and asparagus, tomatoes and onions, cantaloupe and cucumbers. In the last years of her life, as she was battling a heartless cancer, she took classes from the University of Minnesota to become a Master Gardener. I am grateful for her courage and witness to faith as a lifelong learner.

In addition to Grandpa and Granny O., there are others for whom I'd like to share words of thanks. My gratitude extends to my father who taught me a love for the soil and gardening. From an early age I saw him, after a long day of work, come home and tend the garden in our backyard. One of my most cherished childhood memories is planting seeds with him. Dad taught me how to till, plant, water, weed, and wait for a harvest.

As a child, it was my mother who took the bounty from the garden and transformed it into wonderful meals that fed and nurtured the family. She did this on top of raising three children, conquering mountains of laundry, and keeping track of a thousand details. Thank you, Mom, for all of your love and care, which remains the backstory of my life.

These days, my gardening partner is also my life partner, Katie. Though we tend to different areas of the yard, we share in the dream and work of transforming the space out back. At times we are in different places, but that is what makes it fun, fulfilling, and has shaped our yard into something that is unique. Katie exhibits the skill, hard work, and determination of her mother and her grandmother. My wife is a strong woman full of grace and love. I'm deeply grateful for Katie's generous sharing of both with me and our family.

The line drawing of a dandelion on the cover was created by my son, Mark, who is already a gifted artist. My friend, Casey Fuerst, an incredible designer and owner of Tic Tac Toe Marketing incorporated Mark's drawing into the cover design. Thank you both for your willingness to share your talents.

I am grateful to Dr. Gary DeKrey for his review and editing. Your friendship and honest feedback are greatly appreciated as it continues to make me a better writer, preacher, and person.

I appreciate the opportunity that I've had since I was ordained in 1997 to serve two dynamic congregations: Faith Lutheran in New Providence, New Jersey, and St. James Lutheran in Burnsville, Minnesota. You all have shared your wisdom about scores of things both ecclesiastical and biological. Thank you for all that you have taught me along the way. Sharing life together, we have learned much through both ordinary and extraordinary experiences.

HOW DO I USE THIS BOOK?

I have designed this book to be a flexible resource for individual devotional use as well as use in small group discussions in congregations.

Lent: This book can be read as a devotional from cover to cover at any point during the year. You can also choose to read it during the liturgical season of Lent. If you start on the First Sunday in Lent, reading a section a day will take you to Easter Sunday. Appendix A outlines a Lenten reading schedule for you to follow.

Daily Online Component: Appendix B contains information about how you can sign up to receive the book's content through a series of daily emails sent automatically to your inbox in time for your morning coffee. With the purchase of this book, you receive free access for you to the online component.

Resource for Small Group/Book Study: You can also use this resource in a six-week small group or book club setting. I have developed a group Bible Study to accompany the readings, which can be purchased separately through LightFromThisHill.com. The ACCOMPANIMENT EDITION also provides links to video teaching content for each session.

INTRODUCTION

ON PARABLES AND BACKYARD CARE

“When he was alone, those who were around him along with the twelve asked him about the parables. And he said to them, 'To you has been given the secret of the Kingdom of God, but for those outside, everything comes in parables; in order that they may indeed look, but not perceive, and may indeed listen, but not understand; so that they may not turn again and be forgiven.'”

-Mark 4: 10–12

Life is busy and our schedules are packed. Sometimes you go to church; sometimes you don’t. Sometimes your spirit gets what it needs; sometimes it doesn't. Your experience isn’t unusual. Our spiritual lives need care but it doesn't seem like we have the time. Even if we were able to carve out some space, where do we start? Working on increasing our spiritual health can be overwhelming.

Like a backyard in springtime, there is so much to do: removing winter debris; seeding grass in the bare spots; planting vegetables and flowers; mulching; and pruning trees. We need to sharpen our vision and make plans. Where do we want color to bloom and brighten? We need to pay attention to our surroundings. Where will the sun appear and what will remain in the shade? We need to consider how we will use our backyard this season. Will we have a party and expect guests? Will we need space for a swing set for children? How much will we be home this year to enjoy our efforts? How much time, energy, and money are we going to invest? Plans and considerations all make demands upon us. They all require brain space and time.

Of course, we could just ignore the backyard. That is always an option. Put it on the backburner until we have a free moment. It is a strategy that ought to come with a warning label. Caution: If you avoid the backyard, spring will still come. Growth and life will happen in the space behind your house whether you are ready for it or not.

If you put backyard tending too far down on the "to-do" list, then there will be chaos in the form of weeds, critters, clutter, and general disorder. Instead of a space for relaxation and respite, unkempt backyards generate other feelings – disorder, guilt, anxiety, unsettled, and out of control.

Our spiritual lives need our care as much as our backyard. It may not seem like we have the time, energy, or know-how to tend to our spirits. It is certainly easier to put our spiritual care on the back burner. Our culture actually encourages such procrastination with constant messages advocating for immediate gratification. Despite the empty promises that distract and deceive, spiritual care is not a one-time draught from a magical amulet. Spiritual care needs our daily attention among the noise, ups, downs, and busyness of life. We need to stop, breathe, dwell in words and stories about God, reflect, and pray.

Common. Memorable. Simple in structure. Short in length. In each of the Synoptic Gospels (Matthew, Mark, Luke), parables offer the representative content of Jesus's teaching ministry. Jesus teaches in parables. It is his style and modus operandi to use "down-home" examples to provide profound insight into the mysterious Kingdom of God.

The parables of Jesus invite movement in the direction of transformation—from death to life, confusion to clarity, despair to hope, and ignorance to wisdom. These short, insightful lessons about God's Kingdom create a space in which ordinary life can change. They invite believers and non-believers alike to consider anew, weigh alternatives, and respond. Parables welcome dreamers and doubters alike to participate in what God is doing. Purposely open ended, they excite imagination.

What is a little disconcerting, though, is that Jesus's teaching in parables has the stated effect of keeping some hearers in the dark. Some look but do not perceive. Some listen but do not understand. The result? They remain in their ignorance and defiance of the Kingdom of God. They stay spiritually disconnected.

With Jesus's parables, there is a paradox. On the one

hand these “teaching gems” open the heart, mind, and soul to the ever-present, abundant Kingdom of God. The parables make it possible to catch a glimpse of the hidden mysteries of God’s essence. In so doing, they open a door, crack open the window on understanding, and invite us into a place that we could never imagine existed.

On the other hand, parables divide and shut out. The doors are slammed shut and bolted tight. A division of knowledge, connection, and relationships occur that is severe. Parables separate. The two poles of the paradox couldn’t be further apart.

As a teacher and preacher of God’s grace, I find that this separation bothers me. But then I think about my faith journey with its ups and downs; and a little clarity enters the picture. What if the separation of “getting” or “not getting” the parables is merely a description of the spiritual life? What if we are both the ones to whom God gives the secrets of the Kingdom and the ones who are outside? What if the parables are not about dividing people into groups but rather speak to the struggle within each of us between trust and doubt? Parables expose the conflict within as well as outside of us.

The parables lift up the prayer: “I believe, help my unbelief!” They leave us scratching our heads wondering; what does it mean for the tiny mustard seed to grow into a bush large enough for birds to find shelter in its branches? The parables offer an alternate lens and counterpoint to the unquestioned wisdom of the world. They also hold up a mirror and say, “Look, knucklehead, you are not getting this; you are missing what lies right in front of you!”

Parables can open a dialogue within that may or may not be productive at this point. Parables also can cause us to be silent—to stop talking for a moment and listen for the wisdom that begins once we cease our incessant chatter.

This book consists of forty devotionals that come right from the ordinary space of my backyard. It contains original parables of my creation. Through reflecting on ordinary things, I seek wisdom about extraordinary ideas such as forgiveness, grace, and God’s love. I wonder what we can learn from considering bird feeders and raised garden plots, weeds and Tiki torches, compost bins and solar lights, rhubarb and mowing grass? How is the Kingdom of God like these things? What insights can we glean from such everyday stuff?

It is my wish that the few minutes a day that it takes you to pause, breathe, read, and reflect will be a positive step in your spiritual care. I pray that God might bless this effort in such a way as to make our spiritual "backyards" bloom with good things, insights, inspirations, and renewal. To God be the growth and glory of our living!

Accompanying each parable is a prayer and a question to ponder. The prayers vary between being in the singular and plural tense. When we pray, we are always in the spiritual tension of being an individual believer and being a part of a community of believers. The questions that I pose for you to ponder, on the other hand, are asked of you. What do you think? I ask these questions not because I have all the answers—I don't. I want, however, to spark your imagination as the reader. It is after all, my intent to shine a little light on your path.

CHAPTER ONE
THE SPACE OUT BACK AND WITHIN

"I praise you, for I am fearfully and wonderfully made. Wonderful are your works; that I know very well. My frame was not hidden from you, when I was being made in secret, intricately woven in the depths of the earth. Your eyes beheld my unformed substance."

Psalm 139: 14–16a

Behind my house is a small patch of earth. It contains a tiny vegetable garden, a few trees, a birdbath, a patio, and a deck. Though it wouldn't win awards in any gardening magazine, it is a special place—an oasis. In my backyard sanctuary, I find renewal, respite, and relaxation.

Because I live in central Minnesota, my backyard lies dormant through the long months of winter. During this time, the hue changes from green to brown. Unless, of course, snow covers. Then it is white for months. When my backyard is in its white or brown forms, it appears to be barren.

It is absent the flowering bushes, a canopy of leaves, blades of grass, and pots of flowers; the space looks lifeless. Gone are the butterflies and songbirds that flit along their erratic flight paths. Missing is the sweet fragrance of herbs carried by a gentle breeze. The deck chairs, covered with either fall's debris or winter's fallout, no longer offer the invitation to sit and rest awhile. Even the fire pit and grill go unused; covered in tarps and snow, they wait for warmer days.

Surveying my backyard without its lush and leafy splendor, I find myself in the season of waiting. It is hard for me. I quickly become impatient when I sit around. No matter how hard I try, I am powerless to fast forward time. The earth's planetary rotation around the sun pays no mind to my puny desires. Unable to speed up the course of the cosmos, I resign myself to wait.

It is a holy time. Confronted by my inability and its accompanying vulnerability, I am humbled. Pretensions melt away in the face of such reality.

In this chapter, we start our parable-guided journey in the restless place that longs for transformation and signs of new life. Here the physical nature of my backyard collides with the metaphysical essence of my soul. We will look beneath the surface of both landscapes with sacred wonder.

Gardens don't just happen. They begin with a dream and emerge over time. The cooperative exchange between vision, hard work, and nature creates something unique and special.

I challenge you, as I have done myself more than once, to take a closer look. With imagination, look beyond what your eyes behold. Underneath the frozen crust of earth lies a microscopic world that is full of potential. It waits for the right conditions, temperatures, and rainfall. Like the faithful do for the Kingdom of God, the backyard longs for what is yet to come. Though nothing in life is inevitable, conviction fuels the anticipation of what the space might become. What it must become. What it will become.

With imagination look also beyond what you see in the mirror. What lies hidden behind the facade that you present to the world? Where is the truth that is you? Where is the child of God that is underneath the pretensions and constructions of our insecurities, vanity, and insatiable indulgence?

What do you need most? Where do you yearn for healing? What meaning do you seek in your life?

There is a beauty of winter that is often missed by those who dread and slog through the season. Shadows stretching out across the snow are good fodder for reflection. Mary pondered at the crude manger at the news that her baby was part of God's larger plan of restoration, renewal, and resurrection. Looking at the stark landscape behind my house, I yearn for this ability. I seek wisdom about things that are too great for my mind to comprehend and my heart to contain. Though I can't begin to fathom such wonders, I desire them. I long for transformation; I wait for God to reshape and reform my being.

Beloved child of God, there is also a beauty within us that is often missed as we scurry through daily routines and navigate crises. We are quick to believe the lies of a commercial culture that tell us that we are not good enough, smart enough, or beautiful enough. Playing on our insecurities, others tell us that we need their products and praise to matter. Listening to these incessant voices, we stop paying attention to God's message of love and acceptance. We forget that meaning and purpose cannot be manufactured or marketed. Instead, these things come from God and they can be found as we live into our God-given identity as a beloved child who was created to live in communion with God and others.

Potential. Opportunity. Growth. These words come to me as I look out through the frozen panes of glass that separate me from a yard that is sleeping. I dream and imagine the new life that will come to pass in due season. For my yard—an oasis. For my soul—illumination.

Five Parables on Longing

The Parable of the Coffee Mug:

The Kingdom of God can be compared to a mug of morning coffee that you can hold in your hand while you sit on your deck. With a slight refreshing chill in the air, your hands welcome the warmth that radiates from the ceramic container. The aroma opens your senses. A sip of the steaming hot fluid awakens your body as a new day unfolds before you.

A Question to Ponder:
What rituals help you to center, focus, and greet each new day as a gift from God?

Prayer:
Gracious God, awaken my senses. At the start of this day, open within me a space for your creative spirit. Fill me with your love so that I might be a vessel to carry your compassion, hospitality, kindness, and grace to others. Refresh me anew for work in your Kingdom in which I will live, work, travel, and play today. Through Christ, Amen.

The Parable of the Snow-Covered Tarp:

You can also compare the Kingdom of God to a blue tarp that someone used to cover deck furniture for protection before winter. The snow came and blanketed the waterproof barrier, turning its color from blue to white.

Throughout the harsh winter, the trap remained in place. No matter how bad the storm was, how high the snow accumulated, or how thick the ice became, the thin tarpaulin protected and kept everything dry.

A Question to Ponder:

How might you rest in the shelter of God's grace today?

Prayer:

Enduring God, you are the shelter of my life. Protect me from the storms that rage outside my window and within my heart. Let me find in you the courage to push back my fears. Renewed in my strength, inspire me to provide shelter and comfort to others. Through Jesus, Amen.

The Parable of the Dried Hydrangea:

Consider a bed of Hydrangeas along a backyard fence. In the late fall, the multiple flowering lace tops are all dried up. The shrub appears no longer capable of any future glory. There might even be a temptation to cut it down and throw it into the compost bin. Do not be deceived by appearance.

Although the Hydrangea looks lifeless throughout the winter, do not fret. In the spring, the dried-up and inert woody canes will produce leaves and buds. Bundles of flowers will bloom, year after year.

So it is with the Kingdom of God. Do not disregard or discard the Kingdom because it looks dried up. In season, it will grow and flower in places that appear lifeless. Abundant flowering lace tops and broad leaves will flourish from the old woody canes.

A Question to Ponder:

What seems dried up in your life that longs for new growth?

Prayer:

I offer the following prayer for you to use today as you pray at mealtime.

Living God, you bring the gift of life. Enliven this meal with your presence. Bless the food on this table and those who gather around it. Revive our lives so that we might bear the hope of your resurrection in what we do and say. Through Jesus, Amen.

The Parable of the Shovel on the Back Porch:

Get ready; the Kingdom of God is near! Be like the homeowner who puts a shovel outside the backdoor of her house before the first snowfall. Although there were leaves still on the trees in the backyard, she wanted to be prepared for the inevitable arrival of winter.

One night, the snow arrived with a fury. In the morning, a blanket of snow covered everything in sight. After admiring its beauty, the homeowner reached for the shovel that was just outside the door. With it, she shoveled a path through the deep snow on the back deck to the corner of the yard. Her small puppy was grateful.

A Question to Ponder:

What preparations can you make this day to welcome God's Kingdom of love, grace, and peace?

Prayer:

Gracious God, make me ready to welcome your coming. Prepare in my heart a space for love, kindness, forgiveness, and humility. Through Jesus Christ, Amen.

The Parable of the Frozen Ground:

To what can we compare the Kingdom of God?

It is like the frozen ground in winter—hard and solid. Snow-covered, the soil appears lifeless. It is unworkable by human hands. No pick or shovel can turn it over, manipulate it, or cultivate it. No manual strength of ours seems to be able to break through the earth's crust in winter.

Under the frozen layers, there is an unseen movement. As the water in between pebbles, rocks, and soil hardens, it expands. It is strong enough to crush, twist, and upheave. Following ancient and mysterious rhythms, ice moves slowly and deliberately to shape. New possibilities emerge as ice cracks open the strongest of rocks.

Beneath the icy crust, seeds rest, wait, and feel the creative pressure. They keep company with the roots of sleeping trees and dormant bushes. Nothing looks alive or promising. Yet hidden from sight, everything remains vibrant and full of potential. At the right time, spring will come. The frozen ground will thaw and reveal a fresh wave of life.

A Question to Ponder:

What lies hidden within yourself that needs to crack open under the creative pressure of God?

Prayer:

Creative God, underneath the image I project to the world, there are a bunch of insecurities, fears, and worries. Give me the strength today to trust in You. Allow your love to push away the things that keep me from you. In their place, allow your grace to fill me up with new courage, wisdom, and focus. Make me bold in my response to you as I reach out to help and love others. Through Jesus, Amen.

Transforming the Yard: Winter's Sleep

Imagine that it is early April. Even in northern climes, there is a reasonable expectation for spring to be in the air and on the ground. Crocus and daffodils ought to be making their appearance. We ought to be seeing little hints of color and life awakening from slumber—but not this year. Looking out the window, I see a backyard covered with snow. A thick and massive drape of white covers all surfaces. The delights and mysteries of spring are hidden below.

All backyard activity—other than the building of snowmen and a raucous snowball fight—is put on hold. In a manner that is unseasonal, we wait for the seasons to catch up. We wait for temperatures to rise and snow to melt. We yearn for forces beyond our control, outside of our timing, to move of their own accord. There is nothing for us to do but wait and dream.

Gazing upon the snow-covered deck, I see cushion-less chairs stacked together. A smile comes to my face as I think about sitting on the comfy cushions and holding my warm coffee mug in hand. Wisps of steam rise from the full-bodied liquid to meet the rising of sun in the background. In bathrobe and pajamas, I will receive the gift of a new day. I will soon hear the buzz of hummingbirds as they siphon up the colorful, sugary nectar in the feeder, which is now packed away in a storage bin. I might even turn on the fountain or fire table to add additional stimuli to my backyard experience. Fire, water, sun—these things are primal, foundational. I yearn for the sound of a crackle and a trickle. I long to smell the awakening of a new day while holding a warm ceramic cup in my hands.

Looking at the snow-covered yard, I can barely make out the edge of a raised vegetable garden plot. It won't be long until we are able to turn the ground over. Hand tools will eventually break the crust of the soil's winter nap. My wife Katie and I will add rich compost, made from transformed table scraps, to the dark dirt. Everything will be ready for proper planting—more anticipation.

Tress adorned by snow on their branches appear so bare to me. Still, it won't be long until leaves bud and grow. The deciduous woods will come alive again with a thick coat of green providing shelter and shade. Critters great and small will find refuge and food in this space. This critter looks forward to watching the sunlight shimmer as it meanders through the woods.

Dreaming and yearning and waiting are all a part of our lives with God. The changing of the seasons reminds us that instant gratification is the fabrication of an impatient and rebellious creation. According to God's design, life has patterns, rhythms, and seasons. We must wait for timing that lies beyond our control. There is a need for patience. Anticipation bubbles up within for what is to come. We are invited to take a deep breath. Breathe and trust in God's infallible track record to bring about new life in God's own time.

CHAPTER TWO
SOIL

"Other seeds fell into good soil and brought forth grain, growing up and increasing and yielding thirty and sixty and a hundredfold... And these are the ones sown on the good soil: they hear the word and accept it and bear fruit, thirty and sixty and a hundredfold."

-Mark 4: 8; 20

In spring, I run my hand through the soil in my backyard raised garden and smile. The soil is dark and rich. I grasp a hand full of dirt and squeeze. It is moist and cool—ready. With the arrival of Memorial Day, it is finally safe to plant without fear of frost. I can't help but think about the vegetables that will grow in this healthy soil.

In this chapter, I want us to get down and dirty. Inspired by Jesus's parable of the good soil, our focus is going to be on the ground. Without good soil, there is little hope for the kind of growth that leads to an abundant harvest. If we want to have our garden plots and flower beds produce, we need to pay some care and attention to the dirt that fills these areas. Depending on what we are trying to grow, our soil will need certain minerals and nutrients.

My mind wanders from the earth in my yard to the soil of the spirit. What is needed for us to produce abundantly? What makes for the good soil that you can't see because it is found in the innermost part of our being?

Inner soil. From this inside place, which is hidden not only to the world but also most of the time to us, come the ideas, dreams, passions, motivations, decisions, and vision (not of eyes but of the heart). Spiritually this is the place of our most profound connection to and longing for God.

So unique was this place, which the ancient Greeks (such as Plato) called the soul, that it was not even thought to be a part of the body. This idea of body–soul dualism remains popular. You hear some folks say at the time of a funeral that the soul has left the body, which is merely a shell. They find comfort in the immortality of the spirit. Their loved one lives as a spirit away from the body that was crippled and ravaged by illness. For them, resurrection is about a release and freedom from the brokenness of earthly existence.

Personally, I think the ancient Hebrews had a better grip on the situation. They taught that body and soul are not separate but are interactive parts of our whole being. Upon death, we genuinely die—all of us. Death is not an event for opening the release valve on our immortal souls. Death is a time when we as a whole (body and soul) come to the end of our living.

But fear not, this is not a cause of despair. Through the

life, death, and resurrection of Jesus, Christians have hope that at the end of life, God will gift us new life. We confess in worship that we believe in the resurrection of the body...of the whole of our being—body, soul, all of us. Remaining in connection with our whole person, God will transform us beyond our imaginations. Even the deteriorated and crumbled-up bits of our brokenness will be changed into something beautiful and functioning.

Whether we adopt or modify ancient ideas about the relationship between our bodies and souls, I invite you to think for a moment about your essence. What makes you, you? Personality. Life experiences. Wisdom. Aspirations. Ethics. Each of us is wonderfully made and unique in all these categories. If we were to do a soil analysis of each of our lives, the results would come back unmistakably different.

And yet, there would also be a commonality. To be human is to share a similar soul composition. At the center of our lives remains the spark of our created essence—each of us has been formed in the image of God. However hidden it may be, there is something of

God in each person—from Mother Teresa to the most hardened and unrepentant criminals. The challenge is to locate, celebrate, and nurture God's image within us.

There are many ways to rise to this challenge. Each of the world's religions provide well-worn paths that have guided believers over the centuries. For me, as a Christian, this way is found in following the life and teachings of Jesus Christ.

Throughout this chapter, we will use the metaphor of soil to explore the Kingdom of God and the life of discipleship from the inside out. Perhaps it would be better said that we will look at things from the ground up! We will consider our created natures and connection with the earth. How do we honor this sacred link? How do we cultivate the soil and our lives so that they produce good things?

It might get a little messy. You might even get your hands dirty. I'll offer a fair warning: it might also inspire you to do a little planting in your backyard. After all, spring is the season for planting.

Five Parables on Tilling

The Parable of the Mud:

The Kingdom of God is like walking barefoot in your backyard after a saturating rainfall. Transformed by water, the hard earth is now soft and squishy. It sticks to and oozes between your toes.

A slight suction holds each step to the ingredients from which God formed the first human creature. In that nanosecond capture, you are reminded of your createdness. As your foot breaks free, the memory fades, and your walk continues.

Yet, the mud marks and clings to your body. It cannot be denied or forgotten; remember that you are dust and to dust you shall return. You walk onward upon the soft mud as a creature of clay.

A Question to Ponder:

What places remind you of your connection to God's creation?

Prayer:

Gracious God, You created me out of your great love. You shaped my being with great care and precision. I am unique. In all of creation, there is not another body like mine. And yet, I share a connection with all creation. All life bears the mark of its Creator. All life is wonderfully made. Give me the wisdom in my daily walk to appreciate and wonder, honor and respect all life. Strengthen me as a creature of clay to respond as a caretaker of all that you have made. Through Christ, Amen.

The Parable of the Jackhammer:

Listen! A homeowner looked upon an old metal swing set that was in the back corner of his property. It was built a long time ago by the previous owners. For years, the swing set amused and delighted children. Their laughter and joy remained alive in the annals of memory. The homeowner smiled as he recalled the precious recollection.

With appreciation for the past, the homeowner considered the present moment. His children had grown beyond the swing-set years. What is more, the metal toy was starting to rust. Disrepair settled in as a result of disuse. A few of the swing seats were broken. The swing set no longer brought joy but instead was an obstacle. It was in the way of the games that grown children play and posed a challenge to cutting the lawn. What will the homeowner do?

He will remove the swing set by cutting it into pieces with a reciprocating saw. To remove the concrete footings that are buried deep in the soil, he will rent a jackhammer from the local home store. With great effort, he will use the hefty tool to break apart the concrete into small pieces. He will discard the broken chunks and fill the holes with topsoil. The homeowner will then plant grass seed. The backyard space will now be ready for new memories.

So shall it be in God's Kingdom. Those things that no longer bring joy and life will be removed to make room for new possibilities. Rusted obstacles from the past will be taken away so that new spaces are ready for joy to be experienced anew.

A Question to Ponder:

What do you need to remove in your life so that there is a space for new possibilities?

Prayer:

Gracious God, let me be a part of your work of transformation. Help me to identify those things in my life that prevent me from experiencing your love and joy. Let me see the rust and decay of my biases, prejudices, and shortcomings that separate me from others. Give me the courage to move beyond nostalgia and the past so that I may be more present at this moment. Strengthen me to respond in new ways to your life in my life. Guide the hard work of clearing and discarding so that I might plan and plant for what is to come. Through Christ, Amen.

The Parable of the Compost Bin:

The Kingdom of God is like a compost bin that someone put in his backyard to recycle food scraps. Instead of going into the regular garbage and adding to the size and scope of landfills, bits and pieces of organic matter are tossed into the compost bin—orange peels and broken-off ends of asparagus; coffee grinds and paper filters; ash from the fireplace.

They are all thrown together into the container where the process of decay will work its magic. Even the most unseemly piece of rotten lettuce will once again serve a purpose.

Rich soil emerges as aerobic bacteria and organisms work on a microscopic level. Slowly, organic matter is broken down by forces unseen by the human eye. Over time, table scraps are transformed into fertile soil that is used by the gardener to grow more vegetables.

A Question to Ponder:

What parts of your life have decayed and are most in need of renewal and transformation?

Prayer:

God of Transformation, there are parts of my life that are rotten and decaying. Although I try my best, I can't escape the reality of my brokenness. With you, O God, there is hope. Through your great love for me, I am created anew. Your love and grace are always at work in my life, bringing about change and resurrection. Help me to recognize your presence and action in this day so that I might participate in what you are doing. Guide my focus and efforts beyond myself and let me be an instrument of your transformation in the lives of others. Through Christ, Amen.

The Parable of the Dirty Hands:

Once two sisters lived in adjacent houses—one was a gardener and the other was not. Early each morning, the younger sister went out to tend to the soil. There was always something to do in her vegetable garden and flower beds. Within minutes, the sister's hands would become dirty. Although she had multiple pairs of gardening gloves, she rarely used them, preferring to feel the soil between her fingers.

In contrast, the older sister never got dirty. She didn't garden at all and thought it was a waste of her time. Each day she slept while her sister was working outside.

Each year as spring moved into summer, the yards behind the sisters' homes transformed. Green growth flourished in both backyards. That is where the similarity ended.

In the yard of the younger sister, everything was tidy. She mowed the lawn and pruned the bushes. Annual flowers bloomed throughout the season. She would cut small bouquets and give them to neighbors.

Her garden produced cucumbers, peppers, and tomatoes. She also generously shared this produce with others. Year after year, the sister with the dirt under her nails created a beautiful sight to behold.

In the yard of the older sister, there was disorder. Weeds ran wild, and the grass was usually overgrown. Gnarly bushes grew without restraint into distorted shapes.

Without flowers or vegetables, the yard produced nothing for the table or to share with neighbors. By the end of the summer, the yard of the sister with the clean hands was an eyesore.

Everyone who listens to God's invitation to be a good steward will be like the sister with the dirt under her nails. They will rise each morning and tend to the soil, working it until it produces abundantly. They will also be generous and share what they have grown with others. Beauty will accompany them throughout life, and they will be joyful.

A Question to Ponder:

Where in your life do you need to get your hands dirty so that things will flourish?

Prayer:

Gracious God, help me to get started. Motivate me to participate in your creative action that produces abundantly. Give me a generous heart so that I might share with others. Through Christ, Amen.

The Parable of the Considerate Neighbor:

Everyone who follows Jesus's teaching to love others is like the considerate neighbor who enclosed his yard with a chain-link fence. Each morning he would let his large dog out to poop. The dog ran to the fence and sniffed along the edge of the property until he did his business. Later in the day, the considerate neighbor would go out with his pooper scooper and clean up the mess.

And everyone who hears Jesus's words to love others but does not act on them is like the inconsiderate neighbor who also had a large dog but refused to fence in the yard. Each morning, he would let his pet out to answer nature's call. Without a backyard fence, the dog wandered into the adjoining yards. The dog defecated in various places on the lawns and under the bushes of the neighbors. Never once did the inconsiderate neighbor make any effort to clean up after his own dog.

A Question to Ponder:

What would your neighbors say if they were asked about how considerate you are to them?

Prayer:

Gracious God, you command us to treat others as we would like them to treat us. Guide us in our loving so that we might make a difference in the place where we live. Strengthen us to be a good neighbor and to share Jesus's love in what we say and do. Through Christ, Amen.

Transforming the Yard: Digging into the Dirt

The snow is finally gone—melted into oblivion. A collective sigh can be heard as spring arrives in reality and not just on the calendar. The time of waiting is over. Now the work begins. So much needs to happen in the backyard. I need to take the items out of winter storage, brush them off, and set them out. The deck needs another coat of paint. This is just the start of the backyard to-do list. Time and necessity will add things to the list. There will be family discussions and debates about what should and should not be listed. Resources, energy, and diplomacy will all come into play as agendas, dreams, and ideas are sorted out.

For now, however, I just want to stand on the deck (the seat cushions are not yet out—haven't checked that one off the list) and breathe. In early spring, if you breathe deeply enough and inhale with intent, you can smell the dirt itself. It is a thick, earthy (no pun intended) aroma. Musky. Hints of decay mingle with the promise of new growth. It is exciting to smell the first whiffs of dirt after winter's passing. I reach down into the raised garden plot and run my fingers through the ebony soil. Grabbing a handful, I think ahead. As soon as we clear frost's danger, the garden will need to be planted.

Holding the fertile soil in my hand I can't help but think of the divine admonition: remember that you are dust and to dust you shall return. Remember that you are dirt!

Your body contains minerals and nutrients. You are part decay and part promise. You need word and tending. Over time and with nurture and care, you will produce. You have an inkling of harvest in you. In season, you will return enriched, productive, and available to offer yourself in God's ongoing work of creation.

Adam—the name given to the first human creature—means "soil" or "dirt" in Hebrew. According to our ancient stories of creation, the soil is a part of human identity. By the very act of our creation, we are connected to the earth.

Sadly, the human creature has disavowed this biblical truth each time we disregard the earth. We declare ourselves to be more valuable than the sacred soil upon which we tread. We "own" land and property. We destroy mountains and pollute the very ground of our being. We forget that we were created from the dust and to dust we shall return. Failing to remember, we don't show the proper and necessary respect. We shrug off the role of caretaker. Creation moans from our blatant disregard and blasphemy.

Not only have we been harsh on our home planet, but we have mistreated our fellow human creatures. We forget to honor common "ground"—pun intended. We don't see in the other God's soil shaping work. Tribal instincts flare. We demonize, vilify, and disregard those who are different from us. We don't bother taking the time to get to know what lies beneath the surface in another's heart; fear and ignorance subvert this process.

Perhaps it is time for us all to get our hands a little dirty. What if we dug into the soil, sans gloves, and allowed the dirt to remind us of our created being? From the earth, God created you and me. We are connected in our created-ness with each other. We are part of creation, not separate from it. Like the dirt in our backyards in early spring, we wait for the seeds of potentiality to burst open with blossoms celebrating new life.

CHAPTER THREE:
SEEDS

"[Jesus] also said, "With what can we compare the kingdom of God, or what parable will we use for it? It is like a mustard seed, which, when sown upon the ground, is the smallest of all the seeds on earth; yet when it is sown it grows up and becomes the greatest of all shrubs, and puts forth large branches, so that the birds of the air can make nests in its shade.""

— Mark 4: 30--32

The last of the parables in the collection of Jesus's

teaching, as recorded in the fourth chapter of Mark's Gospel, invites us to consider the incredible potential of the Kingdom. Consider the small, insignificant nature of a tiny mustard seed. At first glance, it isn't much of anything—a speck, the tiniest of all seeds. If you didn't know otherwise, you would be hard-pressed to guess that it would amount to much of anything.

Big seeds seem to produce big things. At least that is the mathematics that we usually employ to weigh and judge things. Go big or go home. Size matters. The bigger you are, the louder your voice, the larger your checkbook, the more likely you are to make friends and influence others.

Jesus challenges these ideas. When you think about God's Kingdom, you don't have to think big. In fact, you are closer to the reality when you start small. A tiny mustard seed is a good illustration. Over time, by the grace of God, the tiny seed is transformed into something that produces shelter and shade for vulnerable creatures. It becomes useful and grand.

This should encourage us to take care in our judgments. Do not discard the small things. Do not push away the little things. If you do, you run the risk of thwarting potential shelter and shade. What is more, you run the risk of missing the very Kingdom of God.

Why is this lesson important to Christians?

Christians are as susceptible as anyone to the allure of big and shiny things. We buy into the fallacy that success and grandeur are prerequisites for our time and energy. We overlook, as quickly as anybody, the small things and people in life—sometimes judging them not worth our effort.

If a church is not growing, it must not be doing anything significant. If a person is low on the social or financial totem pole, he or she must not be trying hard enough. The Prosperity Gospel has so saturated our culture that we might even uncritically include that person n our judgmental thoughts that link success with God's favor. Those who are small in success are that way because they are too small in the eyes of God to be noticed, loved, and blessed.

Take care—consider the mustard seed. Even the smallest of all seeds has the potential of growing and offering needed shelter and shade. Don't buy into the lie that is so popular and convenient because it assuages the guilt of those who don't want to share what they have with those in need.

You see, even the tiny mustard seed knows the truth about God's Kingdom. By the grace of God, even small things grow and participate in God's radical hospitality. We grow so that we can offer shelter and shade to those who are vulnerable.

Instead of being disregarded, God has favor on the lowly, the small, and the ones who are judged to be "unworthy." That is the point of most of the parables that Jesus taught. Our belonging to God's life has the implication of discipleship built within it. Disciples care and share the steadfast love of God with others. As a group, we are not about amassing fame and fortune for ourselves. Instead, we are about serving the ones who struggle.

In this chapter, we will be looking at ordinary examples of the potential of God's Kingdom. From stories about dandelions to zucchini and rhubarb, I invite you to consider that we have cause to hope that the future might be different. We need not be trapped forever by our past mistakes or the muck of the present. God is able to bring new, unexpected, and unimaginable life to the places that otherwise appear to be dried up and dead. God's action is mysterious and hidden right in front of our eyes. Christian faith longs for God's coming and the peace, justice, and transformation that it brings.

Five Parables on Sowing

The Parable of the Dandelion:

The Kingdom of God is as if someone blew the seed head off a dandelion causing dozens of fluffy seed parachutes to scatter over their lawn. Each tiny seed that floats upon the wind will find a way to the ground. It will take root and grow into a dandelion. Soon, the lawn will produce more dandelion flowers.

These flowers will continue to multiply as each dandelion eventually turns into a seed head. With more breath and the wind, additional seed parachutes will also scatter. The cycle continues until yellow-orange dandelions carpet the entire lawn. I tell you, it won't be long until the dandelions leave that yard and multiply throughout the neighborhood.

A Question to Ponder:

How might God be present and working in the things that you label as weeds and disregard as worthless?

Prayer:

Gracious God, your love is contagious. Try as I might to contain your love as a private treasure, it moves me to share with others. Your loving presence will not rest for long. Instead of resisting or limiting or being stingy with your grace, forgiveness, and compassion, motivate me to increased generosity. Strengthen my giving so that others might know of your love through my words and deeds. Let me not stop. Guide my living according to your radical hospitality. Use me to love others—family, friends, strangers, enemies. Through Jesus Christ, Amen.

The Parable of the Squash Blossom:

The Kingdom of God is like a squash seed, which, when planted in a large pot on a backyard deck, will grow into a thick-stemmed plant with large green leaves. The stems will spread quickly until they hang over the sides of the pot. Soon large yellow blossoms will appear. In time, each of these blossoms will turn into a tiny summer squash. The squash will grow bigger with each day.

While the squash is still enlarging on the vine, other blossoms will appear. In time, each blossom will transform into another vegetable. The process will repeat itself throughout the growing season. In fact, some flowers will appear underneath the large leaves and will go unnoticed.

These "hidden" blossoms will produce unseen squash. Sheltered by the large green leaves and camouflaged by the thick vines, these tiny squashes will become enormous vegetables.

When the backyard gardener finally sees what her plant

has produced, she will be amazed and surprised. She will also have so many squashes that she will not know what to do with them all!

A Question to Ponder:

What grows unnoticed in your life because it is small and hidden?

Prayer:

Gracious God, too often I don't think that I'm significant or big enough to make much of a difference. There are other voices that are louder. There are others with more power and position. Still others are more outgoing and have larger networks. I forget the mustard seed. I forget the ability of small seeds to grow into large shrubs and trees. I also forget that I have work to do in your Kingdom—work that is filled with compassion and provides for those in need. Help me O Lord, to remember and respond. I do have agency, influence, and resources that are filled with potential to do great things. Empower me to respond by employing what I have in service to you and my fellow humans. Through Jesus Christ, Amen.

The Parable of the Rhubarb:

A young man went to his uncle's garden. At the edge of the older man's yard, there stood a large patch of rhubarb. Through decades of the uncle's gardening, the rhubarb grew and grew. The green leaves of the rhubarb were as large as the ears of an African elephant. The red stems of rhubarb were as thick in diameter as a quarter. Each rhubarb harvest from his patch produced dozens of pies and jars of jam.

The uncle invited his nephew to divide and take a few rhubarb roots for his own garden. With a spade and bucket, the younger man carefully extracted the coveted perennial. He brought home the roots and gently planted them in a section at the edge of his garden.

For the next two years, the young man nurtured the rhubarb plant, allowing it to slowly increase in size. He refrained from harvesting the tiny stalks, which were no thicker than a pencil. Instead, he added manure and compost and allowed the rhubarb to grow. He was patient in his waiting.

In the third year after the transplant, the young man finally picked a few stalks of rhubarb to make his first pie. Over time, his patch became as full as his uncle's patch. From uncle to nephew, the legacy of rhubarb continued in the family. Each year, that same plant produced an abundance of the sought-after fruit-like treasure, which was made into the most beautiful and tasty pies.

A Question to Ponder:

What in your life needs your patient nurture so that it can grow over time?

Prayer:

Gracious God, nurture me in your steadfast love so that I might grow as your child. Root me in your justice so that I might pursue right relationships with everyone I meet. Settle my restless soul in you so that I might dwell in your shalom. Through Jesus Christ, Amen.

The Parable of the Acorn:

What then shall we compare to the Kingdom of heaven? What parable should we use? It is like the first acorn that falls from the tree in late summer. Thud. From a place high on the oak tree, this small nut crashes unto the backyard deck. It hits hard enough to make a sound, then rolls ever so slightly after impact. The first of many acorns to fall, it is a sign of things to come. This marks the beginning of a changing of seasons. Soon, dozens of acorns will follow; there will be so many that the homeowner will have to sweep them on a daily basis to walk on the deck.

What does this parable mean?

The Word of God is the acorn. From above, it breaks into our everyday lives as both a sign and a promise. It is a sign that the Kingdom of God is at hand. As we live life, we will receive more and more reminders of the close nature of God's Kingdom. God's Word not only points to the presence of the Kingdom but also to its power of transformation. God's Word of promise and hope changes our lives whenever it is heard and taken to heart. When we respond to the call for justice and peace, boldly proclaimed by God's Word, we participate in the change God is bringing to bear on our broken lives. Let those with ears listen!

A Question to Ponder:

Where in your life do you see God at work?

Prayer:

Gracious God, change me. Open my heart in those places where it is closed. Forgive my hardness and terseness as I lose patience with others. Replace my impatience, self-centered nature, and prejudice with your love and hospitality. Align my life and values with your grace so that I might participate in your Kingdom that has broken into this world through the life, death, and resurrection of Jesus Christ. Through Christ, Amen.

The Parable of the Surprise Seeds:

There once was a father who loved to garden. Each night, after he came home from work, he tended his vegetables that grew in his backyard. Most of the plants he grew from seed, starting some indoors in plastic trays. Still others he planted directly into the soil.

Every year the amateur farmer ordered his seeds from a catalog. He did this in the waning days of winter when the snow was still covering the ground. With anticipation, he scanned the pages of the catalog looking for the plants that would work best in his garden. It always took some discernment before he placed a seed order.

The father had a son who enjoyed working with his father in the garden. Together they would care for the plants at each stage of growth. With hoes and watering cans, they weeded and watered all through the summer.

One year, when the seed catalog arrived, the father noticed that kids could get a package of mystery seeds for a penny. The son was excited and offered to pay for the package all by himself. When the father's seed order arrived, so did his boy's mystery seeds.

The son opened the package of seeds with great wonder. Inside the paper envelope were a variety of sizes and colors. Carefully, he shook the packet into his hand. The son had a hard time counting all the seeds! He couldn't wait until it was time to plant them. Only then would he know what he was growing—the process was exciting.

Although the arrival of planting season tested the young boy's patience, it eventually arrived. Soon the son planted all of his mystery seeds in the ground. Each night when the father came home from work, the two gardeners went to work: watering, watching, and weeding. Within a short time, the first sprouts appeared.

The rows that the Father planted were uniform and straight. You could see the result of years of practice sowing. The furrows were straight and in order. Each row was marked with a little sign so that when the sprouts appeared, he would know what kind of plant it would become.

On the other hand, the rows that the son planted wandered. Although he followed the same procedure of stretching a string from end to end of the growing space to lay out the seeds in a straight line, inexperience and exuberance caused his line to waver.

The son planted the seeds in the crooked furrows without regard to variety; big seeds were next to small seeds. He didn't bother marking the rows because he didn't know what he had planted. Still, the son looked upon his garden with the same hopeful pride as the father viewed his own.

Weeks passed and both gardens grew; the father and the son continued their nightly regimen of watering, watching, and weeding. Throughout the summer, the plants flourished. The father's plants did so in order while the son's plants remained in disarray.

In due time, blossoms appeared on the vegetable plants. Tiny white and yellow flowers announced to the patient backyard farmers that some vegetables would develop. Sure enough, they did! Among the orderly rows that the father planted, edible delights were abundant. Night after night, baskets of fresh vegetables waited for him to harvest.

Vegetables also appeared in the son's garden. The sense of mystery continued as the boy searched each night among the disorderly and variant leaves. It was unknown exactly what he would find. One night, the son discovered a few beans. On another evening, the boy found a cucumber. Some of the plants didn't produce anything at all—they were crowded out by neighboring leaves. Within the chaos of the son's garden, disguising themselves as potential veggies, a weed or two escaped pulling.

Although the size, scope, and productivity of the father and son's gardens differed, they shared precious things in common. Both enjoyed the contact with the soil that the experience entailed. There was the delight and satisfaction that come from nurturing and growing something. Gardening together also brought both the parent and child closer together in their relationship. Each experienced a vegetable harvest. A bonus for the son was the whole mystery and wonder of it all!

A Question to Ponder:

What role do mystery and wonder play in your life of faith?

Prayer:

Mysterious God, you are bigger than I can even begin to imagine. You are higher than the mountains and farther than the most distant star. Let me dwell on the wonder and mystery of your existence so that awe fills my being. When I reach the capacity of my limited imagination for your majesty and grandeur, remind me that you are as close as my next breath. Create within my heart a deep reverence for both your transcendence and your intimacy. Through Jesus, Amen.

Transforming the Yard: Seeding the Beds

Standing on my deck with a cup of coffee in hand, I look over at the garden box. A few years ago, my sons and I built it as a Mother's Day project for my wife. Each year we have added reclaimed earth to our compost bin. Looking at the black soil, you can almost see the nutrients.

It is a good garden space, the best we could find in our shaded backyard. I would have liked a spot with a little more sun, but nothing is perfect. The sooner we stop our insane search for an elusive perfection, the quicker we will be happy. Enough sunshine makes its way through the tree canopy to shine on the garden box to produce enough vegetables for our table.

I look at our small garden. At this point, it is not much—just a large box of dirt. The Lichtenberger's cat, Celia, perches herself on the edge of the wooden frame. She, too, scans the yard that is starting to come to life. Small buds appear on the trees and shrubs. The crocuses are in the last stage of their short lives. Other bulbs—daffodils and such—have broken the surface with green shoots of their own. Celia watches in silence for the creatures that scurry across the recently thawed ground.

Although my garden box appears to be a lifeless repository of earth, I smile with secret knowledge. There are seeds hidden from view. Beneath the surface lies nature's packages of potential life. Although I can't see the subterranean action, I know that things are in motion. Germination is underway, and it gives me hope as to what is yet to come.

Hope is an integral part of our spirituality. It gives us the needed encouragement that life is more than what we can see with our eyes or construct in our minds. Hope comes as a gift from God, and it creates within our spirit a sacred workspace.

Hope germinates in a variety of conditions because it is so resilient. Down in the deepest and darkest places of our soul where our harshest of judgments prevent us from accepting God's mercy for ourselves, God has planted the hope-filled seeds of forgiveness. When these tiniest of embryos crack out of their shells, they invite us to consider and pursue new possibilities. Suddenly, we have the gift of a future that is not constrained or limited by our past.

Hope also finds germination in seeds of justice and peace. Long the dream of God for all creation, these kernels have been sown over the centuries. In a world where violence, fear, and hatred separate and divide people, the seeds of justice and peace remain underground. Hidden, they await the warmth of all those who wait in hope. Prophets, sages, and seekers long for the time when the tender shoots will break through hardened surfaces.

I join their sacred yearning as I finish my morning coffee. Hope fills me up and warms the innermost parts of my being. Looking at the place where I will plant the seedling that I purchase at local nurseries, I can't help but imagine the garden. It will produce not only a harvest of vegetables for my table but serve as a powerful metaphor of God's future of a return to Eden's glory.

CHAPTER FOUR:
LIGHT

"[Jesus] said to them, 'Is a lamp brought in to be put under the bushel basket, or under the bed, and not on the lampstand? For there is nothing hidden, except to be disclosed; nor is anything secret, except to come to light. Let anyone with ears to hear listen!'"

-Mark 4: 21–23

When something is brought to light, it is out in the open—available for us to examine, consider, and make an honest judgment. Darkness hides. Light reveals. Where there is light, there is promise and potential of understanding, wisdom, goodness, honesty, justice, and belief. Where there is light, there is also the possibility of creating new relationships, perspectives, and paths into the future.

In this chapter our guiding parable from Jesus's teaching about God's Kingdom, deals with our handling of the light. What do you do with the light in your life—your wisdom, understanding, etc.? Do you share it? Do you use these gifts in service of others? Do you seek the higher purposes and meaning of life such as justice and truth? Or do you hide these things?

That is a silly thought, isn't it? Hide a lamp under a bushel. Who does that? What good is a lamp if it is hidden? A hidden lamp serves no useful purpose. Why would a sane person but a bushel over a light? At the least, it is a fire hazard; it seems like a waste.

Unless, of course, you want to keep a secret—hide something in the dark that you want no one else to see or know. An uncomfortable truth, perhaps? Is it a bit of information that, if it got out, might taint relationships or have a negative impact on our reputation? Fear motivates deception, secrecy, cover-up, and turning off the proverbial light. The stakes can be high.

Recently, in the news, many secrets have been revealed that have destroyed the reputations of politicians, actors, producers, etc. Tales of sexual harassment, impropriety, and criminal activity have come to light and folks are scrambling to resign, defend, and control the damage. They thought that they could hide their actions in the shadows. But alas, the light has a way of always shining through.

Perhaps that is a bit dramatic for our everyday lives. Still, I'm guessing that we each have a secret or two that we would just as soon keep tucked under a bushel. Maybe it is not so much a secret about our behavior as it is prejudice or bias that we hold in our hearts? What won't you say aloud but instead mutter within? Is it grief or disappointment that you keep and suffer in silence?

The backyard parables in this chapter are designed to inspire some thoughts around how we respond to the light and truth of the gospel in our everyday living. From fire tables to Tiki torches, my parables will seek the wisdom that is found in the place where light pushes against the darkness and clears away the shadows.

Where there is light there is also heat, so we will also spend some time at one of my favorite backyard places—the grill. In all, I will be seeking the courage to pursue truth and the passion that ignites response. I will also wonder about how light can set the stage for life-giving conversations and create uncommon community.

So, are you game? Do you happen to have a match? Let's light this up!

Five Parables of Shining

The Parable of the Fire Table:

The Kingdom of God is like a fire table on a patio. When it is turned on, the flames dance over the lava rocks (or glass beads). Its warmth and light set an atmosphere that is inviting for friends and family to gather around. When off, it waits with great potential. All it takes to activate it is the turning of a valve and the ignition of a spark.

A Question to Ponder:
Where can you shine the light of friendship today?

Prayer:
Gracious God, burn in my heart the flames of your compassion. Ignite within my spirit a passion for life. Let me see by your light the truth of your love and care for all people. Illumine a space in the darkness of fear, prejudice, hatred, and separation so that I might be able to see a path toward peace, reconciliation, and hospitality. Through Christ, Amen.

The Parable of the Grill:

Early in the day, a man invited his friends to an evening BBQ. It was a last-minute, informal invitation. His friends said they could come and offered to bring a side salad. The man went to the store and bought charcoal, steaks, asparagus, corn, and baby potatoes.

A half hour before his guests arrived, he started his charcoal fire. It took some effort. First, he opened the twenty-pound bag of briquettes and emptied it into a plastic bin. Then, he filled a small chimney with the charcoal. With a match, he lit the old newspaper that he stuffed into the bottom.

He then went to the kitchen and prepared the meal. It only took a few minutes to dust the steaks with seasoning. He put the vegetables in a salad dressing marinade and oiled the baby potatoes with a buttery spray. Patiently, he waited for the coals to turn an ashen orange and glow with heat.

When his friends arrived, it was time to put the meat and vegetables on the grill. Sizzle. Sizzle. The intense heat seared the juices within the steak. Tsh. Tsh. The vegetables made their own pleasing sounds and smells.

The friends gathered around the spectacle of roasting meat and vegetables. Conversations opened and bounced around. Friendships were nurtured and grew as dinner was cooked.

How do you think the man would respond to the question: was it worth the effort?

A Question to Ponder:

When was the last time that you made time to be with friends and family?

Prayer:

Gracious God, you created community and friendships. Thank you for those we care about and with whom we share our lives. Help us to find and make the time to be with them. Strengthen us in the power of hospitality and forgiveness so that we might be generous with our love, companionship, and patience. In the midst of our busy lives, open our circle to include more people in the group that we count as "friends." Through Christ, Amen.

The Parable of the Fireflies:

The Kingdom of heaven can be compared to a summer's evening just after the sun has set. Flashes of light suddenly appear against the violet sky. Random bursts of light shine here and there. Children will rush out with jars to capture the tiny fireflies with their magical bioluminescence. Watching the spectacle brings a joy that is at once elusive and heartwarming. Gleeful children chase insects as the sky darkens. Deep purple turns to black.

Jars with holes in the lids hold the captured bugs that crawl and fly about within the glass containers—unharmed by the incident. Later the thoughtful parents will demand that the fireflies are set free at the end of the night. For the time, however, the fireflies are contained and serve as a source of light within a homemade lantern.

Blink. Blink-blink.

As the children add fireflies, light increases. Each bug contributes to the overall illumination. The glow is at once magical and fleeting—organic and unyielding. Even though the bugs might be trapped in a glass cage, each tiny, yellowish blip pushes back against the night.

A Question to Ponder:

How might you be able to provide a little burst of light to someone who is in a dark place?

Prayer:

Gracious God, burn within my heart with the flames of your compassion. Ignite within my spirit a passion for your life. Let me see by your light the truth of your love and care for all people. Illumine a space in the darkness of fear, prejudice, hatred, and separation so that I might be able to see a path toward peace, reconciliation, and hospitality. Through Christ, Amen.

The Parable of the Solar Lights:

Listen! Those who have ears, listen! A woman wanted to light a border around her yard. The woods that surrounded her backyard were dark and foreboding. It was frightening at night, so she went and purchased six solar lights from the local hardware store.

With care, she pushed each solar light into the soil. Throughout the day, the sun charged the little solar cells. When night came, the solar lights turned on automatically. Although each light was small, together they formed a line of light. Like the function of a child's night-light, the solar lights brought the woman comfort and courage to face the darkness of the night.

A Question to Ponder:

Where could you use a little light to push back your fears and insecurities?

Prayer:

Gracious God, sometimes the night is scary. Darkness hides things. We can't always see a clear path. Fear enters our hearts and we shut down. Shine your light of love in our night. Brighten the space around our hearts so that we might find the wisdom and courage to open up beyond ourselves. Make us instruments of your light so that others might know of your love and care. Through the Light of Jesus Christ, Amen.

The Parable of the Homemade Firestarter:

A resourceful, wise man had an old coffee can under his kitchen sink to save bits of wax. Each time a candle would burn out, he would take the stubs of wax and put them into his can. He'd also scrape melted wax from the bottom of candle holders and add that waste too. Friends would bring him small bags of their wax trimmings. Little by little, the contents of the metal container increased.

At the same time, the wise man also kept the wood shavings and sawdust that he produced in his small garage workshop. For months, the refuse bin grew in volume.

When both coffee can and sawdust bin were full, the wise man set out to make fire starters. Carefully, he placed the metal coffee can on the gas stove to melt the wax. Next, he took paper cups and filled them with sawdust. With practiced precision, the wise man poured the wax into the paper cups. The wood fibers absorbed the molten liquid quickly.

After the wise man used up all the wax in the can, he

allowed the fire starters to cool down. Before long, they hardened and were ready for use.

Later that evening, the wise man took his recycled fire starters outside to his firepit. He placed one of his tiny creations in the center of a pile of sticks, twigs, and logs. Lighting the fire starter with a match, the wise man watched the repurposed materials burn with intensity. He smiled as the fire starter did its job. Over the next twenty minutes, the enduring flame ignited a roaring campfire.

A Question to Ponder:

What can you do to create some light for someone who is in a dark time?

Prayer:

Gracious God, let me not hide your light or love. Give me the courage to shine brightly so that others might know of your care for them. Shine your grace, love, and forgiveness through me. Through Christ, Amen.

Transforming the Yard: Lighting Up the Dark

The mid-sized lantern hangs from a hook over the side of my deck. Inside, it contains a battery-lit, LED candle. The lantern comes on at some point after dark. I haven't quite been able to quite figure out the timing. It seems to have a mind of its own. We have had it for a while, and it seems to not function as it once did. But it still works. At its own time, it will shine. I'll see it from the kitchen as I look out at the otherwise dark backyard. Sometimes it will be on when I head out onto the deck in that pre-dawn time to write—unpredictable.

As I think about it, my unpredictable lantern is not unlike my spiritual life; it gives light and witness to God's love. The light, however, is not as predictable as I'd like. In my heart, I also want to be better at shining. I know that the world, my community, family, and relationships could use a little more brightness.

When I shine my light, it feels good. It gives me satisfaction that makes me smile from the inside out. Shining into the darkness around, I begin to see the faces of others. My light reflects in the dark of their eyes producing a glint. Smiles are contagious. Joy spreads with the light. Soon, other lights emit. The process is organic and viral. Light begets light and allows for seeing, knowing, understanding. When light shines, a community is created among friends, acquaintances, and even strangers.

But my light doesn't always come on. Sometimes, I cower and cover the light source of my life. I get afraid and overwhelmed. At times, it is just pure laziness. When I dwell in the darkness—refusing or unable to shine—something negative happens in my soul. I become withdrawn and unhappy. Joy, itself, seems gone and unattainable.

Without light, I buy into the paranoia that I'm alone in the universe and everything is out to get me. Seeing, knowing, and understanding become elusive. In the extreme, I will be vulnerable to conspiracy theories and tempted to take any means necessary to regain control and self-determination.

Wow, that went south quick, didn't it? And that is just the point—good people can get into dangerous places quickly when they are not clinging and walking in the light of God.

Let's shift our light metaphor for a moment. From a battery-operated lantern that goes on (or doesn't) with a timer, I direct your attention to another light feature of my backyard paradise—Tiki torches.

I'm not exactly sure why, but I'm a sucker for Tiki torches. Maybe it is because I love all things Hawaiian from the slack guitar chords to the loud floral shirts. Perhaps it is because I'm mesmerized by the dancing flame; I'm not sure and it really doesn't matter. I like Tiki torches and over the years have always had them in the backyard.

I like lighting my Tiki torches whenever I sit on the deck at night. Often this happens when Katie and I have company. We will turn on the fire table, a recent addition to our night-time illumination features. The open flames have an energetic dance party. There is something about fire that creates an atmosphere to bring people together.

In the flicker of torches and fires, we see each other in a different light. Maybe we are a little more real in the warm glow of a flame. A little more human? A little less in the manufactured spotlight that highlights the facade we present to the world. Maybe it's just me, but I feel more like myself in the dancing lights of Tiki torches and campfires. I can just be without having to worry about judgment. I find when I'm in this space, I'm more available and relaxed; ready to share life with others. I'm also freed to shine from the heart of my being.

How do you shine? Under what lighting conditions are you best able to be the person who God made you to be? What candles, torches, and fires can you light this day that will help your light shine before others? Time has come to light up. The darkness, confusion, and division of our times need all of God's "lanterns" lowing brightly on a more consistent basis.

CHAPTER FIVE
WEEDING

"The measure you give will be the measure you get, and still more will be given you."

— Mark 4:25

Judgment. Whenever someone brings up the word "judgment," it seems to dampen the conversation. It makes us uneasy. I have also noticed that it seems to divide folks into opposite camps.

On the one hand, the pro-judgment folks seem all too enthusiastic. According to them, what this world, with all of its chaos, ambiguity, and danger needs is a little more hellfire-inspired order. With nostalgic glee, these folks want to return to yesteryear's firm rules about conduct and behavior. They will maintain that we've gotten too soft with our religion. There is too much talk about God's love and not enough emphasis on morality. They want greater accountability—usually from others—in all spheres of life including the sacred.

If the word "judgment" animates those on the right of the spectrum, it has quite the opposite effect from those on the other side. When the word judgment is spoken these folks cringe. For them, grace— God's unconditional love—is, well, unconditional. Everything is forgiven and accepted.

With iconoclastic fervor, these folks want to eliminate judgment altogether. Who is anyone to pass any judgment on anyone else? Ultimately, universal forgiveness makes any conversation about judgment mute.

Forgiveness and acceptance are needed most in our

messed-up world. Instead of building walls, we need to lessen all the barriers that keep people from one another. Fewer rules will allow freedom to purge fears and suspicion. They want greater liberty—usually for the ones on the margins—in all areas of life including the sacred.

Even though neither side readily acknowledges it of the other, both the pro-judgment and anti-judgment sides read and use the Bible. Their interpretative lens and conclusions, however, are so diverse and contradictory. Sadly, each side's engagement of scripture has the effect of increasing the chasm between both positions.

Folks are quick to highlight their favorite passages concerning judgment or anti-judgment. There are enough mutually exclusive passages to go around and widen the impasse. Both sides can quote and debate the whole day long without convincing the other. Wielding the Bible battle-ax will bloody bodies, but it is not likely to win the day.

I could ask you, where do you find yourself in this

sacred struggle? If you really want to tell me, I'd listen. But honestly, I'm not all that interested overall in debating the concept of judgment with you. Here's why. Discussion of judgment will eventually get to the whole issue of salvation.

Many Christians obsess about what will happen when they or their loved ones die. Will they go to heaven or hell? What is the eternal judgment that God will hand down upon their souls? Worry and angst barge into hearts struggling with these questions. Souls obsessed with these dark, disturbing thoughts are more likely to shut down and turn inward than they are to open up and risk loving others. From my experience as a pastor, hell-inspired thinking can lead to separation and unbridled judgment of others.

What I would rather talk about—and where I will be heading with this chapter's parables—is the favorable role judgment and accountability can play in our spiritual lives alongside the ever-present abundance of grace. I will be staking out the middle ground between the poles of judgment and mercy.

I need to raise a warning flag. There is a good chance that I might disappoint you. If you have firmly planted your feet in either the pro- or anti-judgment group, then you may not like where I'm heading.

If you are a brimstone aficionado, you will notice that I leave the back door open. Salvation is not of our doing and will always come as the abundant and reckless gift of God. The fires of hell burn but the waters of grace are sufficient to put them out.

On the other hand, if you are an "anything goes" and "everything is good" sort of person, you will notice that I will be lifting up the rule of love as a guiding principle that comes with accountability and responsibility. Love is, after all, the rule of Jesus. Christians are accountable on the basis of love. Love mandates, guides, and forbids. "Anything does not go" because everything is not loving.

Unloving words and actions are inconsistent with the life, death, and resurrection of Christ. Hatred of any sort is not good and deteriorates the spiritual health of individuals and church communities. We need to be on our guard against both the overt and less obvious forms.

I seek balance and a positive application of judgment in spiritual living. This is what Jesus does. Parables that might seem at first glance to advocate harsh judgment are alongside parables that speak of abundant grace. I think that this is on purpose. Jesus invites us into the paradox of faith. For the law-loving Pharisee (in all of us), Jesus's parables pull in the direction of God's overwhelming forgiveness. For the freedom junkie (again, in all of us), Jesus's parables pull us toward greater accountability and action.

So this is the "judgment" chapter. The parables that lie ahead will challenge us to follow Jesus's mandate to love the other—family, friends, neighbors, acquaintances, strangers, and even the enemy. They hold up a mirror so that we can look at our unloving selves and do some critical reflection. Implicit in them is the call of repentance and God's promise of forgiveness. We are invited to turn anew to the love of God and allow it to transform.

It's going to be hard and, at times, might even border on harsh. Are you willing to sit on the edge of the garden plot, like the Lichtenberger house cat, Celia—embrace rather than discard? Can you allow these everyday illustrations to inform your faith and provide some balance?

For the gardeners among us, this is the difficult work of weeding.

Five Parables of Uprooting

The Parable of the Worn Deck:

Pay attention to what you hear!

What does the homeowner do with an old, worn-out deck? I tell you, she will take the time, energy, and effort to sand it down, board by board, and repaint it.

Or she will tear it up and replace the boards with new material made of composite plastic that doesn't weather. The homeowner will not allow the worn-out deck to rot in place and fall apart because it poses too high a threat to her family.

So it is with the Kingdom of God. The old and worn-out parts shall be rejuvenated or replaced.

A Question to Ponder:

What parts of your life have worn out and need your attention?

Prayer:

Gracious God, be present to me in the worn-out and broken places of my life. Forgive me where I have not loved or cared for others. Renew my worn-out spirit so that I might find new strength to live as you would have me live. Guide me anew in the paths of your grace so that I might participate in your justice and peace. Through Christ, Amen.

The Parable of the Nesting Material:

Be willing continually to share what you have with those in need; be like the woman who fills a small wire cage in her backyard with bits of yarn, cotton fluff, and small twigs.

Finches come and take these materials in their tiny beaks. They fly away to build their nests. As the contents of the cage are diminished, their nests grow as places to shelter eggs and vulnerable offspring.

After a rainfall, they seem to return for fresh bedding. The woman, who will keep the cage full of dry and soft materials, remains diligent in her efforts throughout the season.

I tell you, her efforts to provide for the tiniest of creatures will not go unnoticed by the Creator of Finches and people.

A Question to Ponder:

In what ways might you contribute to the shelter and safety of others?

Prayer:

Gracious God, you provide for all creation. Make me aware today of both your care and provision. Each breath I take comes as a gift. Each occurrence of shelter, food, warmth, family, and protection comes as blessings. As I am grateful for these things, make me aware of those who have less and are in need. Empower generosity within me so that I might share what I have with others. Let me be a conduit of your grace and love so that others might sing your praises. Through Christ, Amen.

The Parable of the Deer Buffet:

One day a foolish man went out into his backyard to plant a garden. He built a raised bed garden box. Back and forth he went to the home store to buy bags of topsoil and flats of plants.

After filling the garden box with dirt and raking it smooth, the man planted; he put in tomato and pepper plants. Carefully, he sowed rows after rows. He planted lettuce from a package of seeds. Around the border, he even put a set of onions. After much hard work, he surveyed his garden and was satisfied with all that he had done to make it as he wanted.

Days passed by; each morning, the man looked at his garden with pride. He watched as tiny white blossoms formed on the pepper plants and yellow blooms appeared on the tomato plants. Soon he would reap a harvest of vegetables.

During the night, however, the deer came into his unprotected yard. Undeterred, they feasted upon the blossoms and tender leaves. In the morning, the foolish man saw that his garden had been invaded. He was devastated as he looked upon the ruined plants.

So it will be with all those who work hard and yet don't take steps to safeguard what they have planted. The wise not only plant but they also protect the tender shoots and blossoms so that they might grow.

A Question to Ponder:

What are the tender shoots and blossoms of your faith life that need protection and attention?

Prayer:

Gracious God, I thank you for your blessing and presence in my life. The gift of faith that you have given me is precious and fragile. So much in this world threatens its growth and its potential to bear fruit. Guard and strengthen me in your grace and love so that I might withstand the challenges and threats to my spirit. Give me the wisdom to tend my soul each day in prayer and devotion to you. Embolden my response so that I live my life with openness and trust. Send me out with renewed zeal to care for others. Through Christ, Amen.

The Parables of the Deck Box and Weed Puller:

Listen! Let those who have ears hear. Wake up and take action, for the Kingdom of God is at hand.

Be like the wise person who takes in the seat cushions from all the deck chairs each night. With great care, he puts the cloth seats and pillows into the waterproof deck box, making sure that they are not left out. When the rain falls during the night or the dew falls in the morning, the cushions remain dry.

Or be like the conscientious weeder who carefully scans the garden every few days, looking for weeds. When she sees a weed, she pulls it out immediately. I tell you, she will not let weeds grow and crowd out the good plants.

A Question to Ponder:

What relationships in your life do you most overlook or take for granted?

Prayer:

Good and gracious God, help me stay active and tend the garden that is my faith. Keep me ever aware of your love and the claim that it has on my living. Guide the way that I relate to others so that my actions, words, and thoughts might reflect your grace, hospitality, and forgiveness. Empower me to participate in the creative and redemptive work of your Kingdom. Through Jesus Christ, Amen.

The Parable of the Marigolds and Vegetables:

To what shall we compare the Kingdom of God?

It is like a wise woman who planted marigolds between the rows of vegetables in her garden. Her friends found the unusual agricultural practice strange and unsettling. She was the only one they knew who mixed flowers with peppers and tomatoes. The neighbors talked about her without kindness. They judged her to be a misguided freak. She was labeled a "radical" who sought to dismantle tradition in favor of new-fangled and dangerous ideas. What was next? Did she plan to eat the flowers?

The wise woman disregarded the chatter. Instead of defending herself, each morning, she tended her garden and delighted in its growth.

Before long, the neighborhood gossip shifted to outright envy. Although the neighbors were reluctant to admit it, her garden outshone all the others. Not only were the flowers pleasing to the eye but the marigolds kept away most of the bugs.

The only insects to visit the wise woman's garden were the bees that helped to pollinate the crops of nearby farms. Although all her critics needed to use toxic chemicals to ward off pests, the wise woman's garden remained organic.

At harvest time, there was no question as to whose garden produced better-tasting vegetables. There was also no question about which garden was most beautiful.

A Question to Ponder:

Where do you find yourself close-minded or not open to new ideas?

Prayer:

You can use the following prayer today as you pray at mealtime.

God of all, you have richly blessed creation with wondrous diversity. Thank you for the bounty of food to which we have access and which we can enjoy. Bless the food upon this table so that it might strengthen our bodies and allow us to celebrate differences. Through Jesus, Amen.

Transforming the Yard: Working Hard

It wasn't so long ago that I saw the crocus through the window in my living room that looks out into the backyard. Although they last for a short period of time, the crocus is perhaps one of my favorite blooms. Sure, the flower is pretty unto itself. Its purple and white hues add a bit of needed color to the drab surroundings.

Of greater import, however, is what this small purple blossom represents. Hope. Spring. New life. Gone is the harshness of deep winter. The time for green growth has arrived. Shortly after you see crocuses, you will be overwhelmed by the rapid deployment of spring.

The annual arrival of crocus brings with it a reminder; their tiny, flare-shaped bodies trumpet a call that awakens my lazy self. Gardening season is near, and suddenly there is much work to do!

Throughout this chapter, I shared parables of participation and effort. These were stories of "doing" the work of God's Kingdom. Responding to God's love and grace, we do. Or we do not. There are consequences to both our action and inaction. When we follow in the path of love, we are in alignment with God. When we follow our agendas and inclinations apart from love, we are heading in a different direction. Separation from God occurs; or to use the language of Christian tradition, sin abounds. This has negative implications in our relationship with God and with others.

Although we can't by our work obtain God's favor, earn God's grace, or fashion eternal peace, what we do matters a great deal. God's Kingdom will be known or hidden according to our words, deeds, and responses. We have a role and a part to play. To ignore this reality is to pursue what Lutheran Theologian Dietrich Bonhoeffer labeled "cheap grace." (see Cost of Discipleship).

The reason that my backyard looks lovely these days is a direct result of Katie's many efforts of planting, pruning, weeding, mulching, fertilizing, etc. Were it not for her excellent work, the yard would be unruly. Sure, it might be green, but I doubt there would be as many flowers and we wouldn't be awaiting a vegetable harvest.

I am grateful for Katie's energy, persistence, and

attention. Like the area inside our house, Katie's work has created a home space outside the back door. There is a favorable judgment to be made each time we sit on the deck, relax, and share time with friends.

So it goes with the spiritual life. It takes work. It takes daily attention and care. Prayer, reflection, and engagement in helping others are all part of the good and holy work that is needed. Sure, the harvest will always come as a gift and usually when we least expect it; but hard work matters. Efforts of cultivation make a difference.

Our life with God and with others takes tending, nurture, and care. Relationships grow as we engage with one another. When we ignore, deny, or overlook those with whom we are connected something diminishing happens. Relationships suffer and lie dormant or even die. Our inaction levies an adverse judgment. Sometimes the damage is irreparable or irreversible. From time to time, we can find ourselves in a hell of our making.

Judged. Broken. Separated. Alone. Hurting. We are all in need of help, reconciliation, reconnection, and grace. Like the person who has fallen into a giant pit, our predicament is made worse by our inability to get ourselves unstuck. Now the work seems futile. Try as we might, at this point in the journey, we find ourselves unable to move forward. Enter frustration and despair.

It is at this moment when we are lost that we are in most need of God's intervention and grace-filled action. The good news, gospel, is that God acts. God's nature is one of redemption. God responds, even when we are unable, to bring about renewal.

Forgiveness is no longer an abstract concept. It is a tangible work of a loving God on behalf of a judged and damaged people. For me (and you) in real time. Forgiveness repairs the bruised and broken connections with the healing balm of love. No matter the tears and gaps in the relationship with God from the past, forgiveness mends and allows for something new for the future.

A crocus breaks through the ground as a sign that spring has arrived. God remains steadfast and faithful. At this point, a new invitation to participate, cultivate, tend, and care emerges. We are given another chance to join in the daily work of gardening. It is never too late for us to take part in the work of the Kingdom. Thanks be to God for the cycles and seasons that surround us and give us hope.

CHAPTER SIX
GROWTH

"The earth produces of itself, first the stalk, then the head, then the full grain in the head. But when the grain is ripe, at once he goes in with his sickle, because the harvest has come."

— Mark 4: 28–29

Abundance. Bloom. Lush. Everywhere you look in my backyard there are multiple shades of vibrant green and splashes of color (white, red, pink, and purples). Hydrangea and peony have grown to the size of bushes and contribute softball-sized flowers as a backdrop to the annuals planted in front. Large green and white leaf hostas line the beds. I can go on with this escalating description of the plethora of beauty that is present in my yard these days. But I will stop. I don't want to risk losing your attention or having your eye roll cause you to lose your place on the page.

It is just when I look outside in this time of late spring (astronomical summer doesn't arrive until late June), it is hard for me not to be effervescent in my descriptions. I am deeply grateful for the growth and plenty that can be seen everywhere in my backyard. I'm sure that I'm not alone in my observations. I bet that your yard is looking great too! Now is the time of the year, after all, that things are growing.

Growth has a mysterious quality. Oh sure, biologists can describe how it happens. We can even capture a second-by-second record of a flower blooming with time-lapse photography and watch it happen. Still, there is something about growth that eludes us. It is almost magical whenever life flourishes. Looking at the beauty and abundance of a garden, I am convinced that there is something more that is happening than just the aggregate sum of biological processes.

That "something more" I like to think of in sacred terms. Growth is evidence of the work of a Creator who remains engaged with creation. When I look at the flowering of a garden, I am filled with sacred wonder and gratitude. Thank you, God, for the beauty that unfolds before my eyes. I say these words in my heart as I witness the Creator in action. What joy there is to embrace with my senses of sight, smell, touch, and taste!

If the last chapter was about "our work" and the need for our participation in the process of cultivation, this chapter is about the mysterious and fantastic quality of God's work. The parables that I share will invite us to honor the life around and within us as a mysterious gift from God. I hope that they will also foster a sense of humility. Only with humble hearts are we better able to care for God's creation.

How do we do this in our everyday living? How often do we stop and give thanks for the blessings of life that surround? Do we pause long and often enough to be in awe of life? Do we espouse values of reverence and humility when we relate to creation? Do we let down our guards and stop trying to control and subdue what God made?

I hope that this chapter's parables will raise these questions among others. May we be surprised and refreshed in the cool shade of the trees in the backyard by the mysterious gift of growth. It is time for us to celebrate the harvest that comes from participating in the co-creating work of God.

Five Parables of Celebrating

The Parable of the Springtime Rain:

The Kingdom of God can be compared to a springtime rain. Suddenly, the sky turns dark. A single drop falls and we hear the sound of it hitting the earth. Then another and another. One by one, multiple drops fall, gradually increasing in volume and intensity.

In a moment, springtime rain surrounds us on all sides. It is like an orchestra that rapidly crescendos. There is an undeniable passion as the heavens seem to open and sheets of water pour upon the earth. Rain at this time of the year is substantial and laden with promise. You can smell it in the air.

This water will quench the thirst of rapidly growing plants and buds. The rain will also sink deep into the ground and replenish the water table, which is sorely needed in advance of late summer drought.

I tell you, even though the rain will eventually stop, its effects will linger and refresh. The experience will be remembered and celebrated.

A Question to Ponder:

What are the dry places in your spirit that are most in need of God's refreshment?

Prayer:

Gracious God, you bring springtime waters that renew the earth. We thank you for the lakes and rivers, ponds and creeks, headwaters and aquifers. From the Red Sea of Exodus to the font of our baptisms, we praise you for the way that you have used water throughout the ages to bear your redemptive purposes. In this day, rain your love upon us. Fill us with forgiveness, grace, and a generosity of spirit. Open our free-flowing response so that we might channel your goodness and gifts to others. Through Christ, Amen.

The Parable of the Bird Feeder:

With what can we compare the Kingdom of God, or what parable will we use for it?

It is like a bird feeder that someone hangs on his or her backyard deck and fills with seeds. Before long, birds will come from hidden places to feed. Different types and sizes of birds will perch upon the feeder and eat. Back and forth, they will fly. Chickadees and robins. Sparrows and wrens. Songbirds of all kinds will gather.

As the bird feeder is filled with more seed, the avian feast shall continue throughout the year. With each bird that comes, the owner of that home is brought a sense of delight and joy.

This is what the homeowners will do, they will hang new feeders. These added feeders will hold various types of seeds to attract more varieties of birds. Cardinals and finches will now arrive. They will even hang a jar of nectar to welcome hummingbirds. With each species that comes to feed, the bird-loving homeowners' joy increases exponentially.

A Question to Ponder:

How can you celebrate the diversity that God has placed into your day?

Prayer:

Gracious God, the source of abundance and diversity, I thank you for your many blessings in my life. Feed me this day with an abiding sense of gratitude. Let me experience life as a precious gift. Give me a healthy sense of humility so that I back away from a sense of entitlement and privilege. Make me generous so that I share rather than hoard what you have given to me. Help me to put my life into proper balance so that I might relate to others with the same kind of love that you have showered upon me. In the process of my grateful living might I bear and bring delight and joy to others. Through Christ, Amen.

The Parable of the Toad House:

There was a woman who bought a cute, mushroom-shaped lawn ornament from a local gift shop. She rushed home and placed it in her garden. It was bright and colorful with a little printed sign that clearly identified it as a "Toad House." The woman wished to provide shelter for the many toads that she found hopping around her yard.

Each day she checked to see if any toads had moved into this small domicile. Each day she noticed that there were no toads in the designated house.

One morning, after checking "Toad House," she noticed an old wooden bucket turned over. When she picked it up, a medium-sized toad hopped out from underneath.

A few days later, the woman checked to see if that toad went into "Toad House." It did not. The mushroom-shaped object was empty. She opened the base of her fire table to turn on the gas ignition. Once again, she was surprised to find a toad in the bottom of the fire table. It hopped away.

The next morning, the woman once again checked "Toad House" for occupants. There were none. Walking to the shed to get the lawn mower, she noticed another large toad in the shade of a large rock. With big eyes and an expanding throat, the creature watched her without moving at all.

So it is with the Kingdom of God. It surprises us by appearing in the times and places where we least expect it. Rarely does it appear according to our designs or well-laid plans.

A Question to Ponder:

Where is the place that you least expect to encounter the love and grace of God?

Prayer:

Gracious God, you surprise me. Sometimes in the strangest places and oddest times, I capture glimpses of your love and grace. When I least expect it, you bring a smile to my heart, and I'm filled with joy. At other times, when I try to conjure up your presence with religious thoughts and incantations, it seems like you are nowhere around. You elude my control. It appears that you refuse to play by my rules and follow my carefully laid plans and manipulations. Forgive my blasphemous attempts to harness your power for selfish desires. Enable me to trust in your presence and providence. Open my spirit so that I am available for your purposes and direction. Remind me that I'm not and I don't need to be the center of the universe. Redirect my energies and efforts outward so that I may be found in the places of hurt, struggle, and restlessness. In the unlikely places of this world and my soul, let me discover you anew. Through Christ, Amen.

The Parable of the Mower:

The Kingdom of God can be compared to a backyard lawn. Throughout the spring and early summer, the lawn grows rapidly; it becomes long, lush, and unruly.

Upon seeing the growth, the homeowner will get out his lawn mower and cut the grass. Even if it takes him more than one pass, the homeowner will mow and mow, until the lawn is trimmed.

The grass will continue to grow, and before long, he will need to repeat the process of mowing. Throughout the summer, even as the days lengthen and the pace of growth slows down, the lawn will require regular tending and great care.

A Question to Ponder:

What examples do we have of abundance from our lives and what do they teach us about God's love?

Prayer:

Gracious God, your Kingdom continues to grow around me. Give me the vision to see and delight in it. Give me the courage to participate in your love and grace. Through Jesus Christ, Amen.

The Parable of the Volunteer Watermelon:

The Kingdom of God is like a gardener who went into the backyard to plant vegetables. With care, she turned over the dirt in a six-foot square garden plot. It wasn't the first time that she planted.

As the experienced gardener incorporated compost and manure into the soil, she smiled with anticipation. Soon the rows of beans, lettuce, and tomatoes would produce a harvest. Everything was in neat and organized furrows. With any luck, the small garden plot would yield enough veggies for herself and her friends. Based on past success, it was a reasonable expectation.

Each morning, the woman went to look at her garden. Gradually, she watched the land come to life. Small leaves sprouted. Careful not to damage the seedlings, she weeded and watered the leaves. Before long, the plants established themselves. In every row that she planted, there were signs of new life.

One morning, during her routine inspection, she noticed an odd plant in the corner of the garden. It didn't fit in any of the rows and wasn't of any variety that she planted. Still, it didn't seem to be a weed. With wonder and a sense of curiosity, the gardener decided to let it grow.

With the same love and care that she gave to all her plants, the gardener tended to the mystery plant.

Before long, the plant revealed itself to be a vine. With fat leaves, it snaked along the edge of the garden and onto the lawn. One morning, the gardener noticed a blossom on the vine. The orange-yellow flower bloomed alongside the crop of beans and with the yellow tomato blossoms. There was an unplanned beauty to it all.

As the yellow flowers on the tomatoes turned into tiny green orbs of fruit, so did the unknown plant's blossom transform. It was bigger and heavier than the other vegetables. Imagine the gardener's surprise when she discovered that a watermelon “volunteered” to show up in her garden!

A Question to Ponder:

Can you think of a time in your life when you were surprised by an unexpected blessing?

Prayer:

Gracious God, I rush through most days like a chicken without a head! Life is busy. There is so much to do; so much that I must do. This confusion and kerfuffle have allowed me to buy into the lie that I alone am responsible for what I have. I have earned the blessings of my life, and it is my every right to keep every blessing close at hand. Give me the wisdom today to see the foolishness in such thinking. Help me to stop, breathe, and be grateful. Increase humility within me so that I might let go of misdirected entitlement and privilege. Forgive my blasphemy of control and stinginess. Create within me a generosity that imitates the love that Jesus has for all people. Redirect my doing so that it is less frenzied and more focused. Teach me to be your child. Through Christ, Amen.

Transforming the Yard: Wonder and Gratitude

It is still mostly dark outside when I pour my morning coffee and make my way onto the back porch. Facing east, I watch the sky as the ceramic cup warms my hands. Things lighten around me. Shades of green emerge as yellow and orange blend overhead with the purple sky. The calls and squawks of a half dozen birds announce the arrival of a new day.

For me, this time on my backyard deck is a sacred communion with life. It is a tiny slice of nature and creation that renews and revives me to the core of my being. Everywhere I look, I see signs of life and growth. From where did it all come?

Sure, Katie's efforts of planting, pruning, and primping are partly responsible. Cal's Market, a local nursery, is another healthy supplier. Favorable growing conditions made essential contributions. But there is something more—more than the accumulation and summation of the parts.

In the sky, the purples have all faded and have been

replaced with a baby blue. There is still yellow in the sky, but now it has turned pastel. The white wisp of clouds can be seen on the horizon. Light has arrived in penultimate fashion. Shadows have all receded. Single leaves and flowers are now visible and ready to be admired or fade into the background of the woods that lie just beyond the backyard fence. Critters can now be seen as they scurry searching for food. Birds soar and dart overhead. Another precious day begins

Sitting with my morning coffee on the deck, I watch with wonder as the sky is now glowing with light. Before my eyes, another day is birthed. Another day begins as the ancient cycle of planetary rotation completes another turn. Facing the warmth and light of the sun, it is time for the day. Today is here. It is perhaps the most precious of all gifts. A day to live—full of opportunity, hope, and promise—lies ahead.

Questions pop into my head as the coffee wakes me up. What do I have to do today? Where will I be going? What will I do in the coming hours? To what do I have to pay attention? A list quickly emerges as I feel my blood pressure rise. It is at this moment, when I am susceptible to shifting into gear, that I need to pause. Sometimes I catch myself. Before hopping onto that metaphorical treadmill and reentering the proverbial rat race, my soul needs some care.

Before I get any further down the path of plotting out my day's doing, I need to stop and breathe. My spirit needs me to take a good look around and see with the vision of my heart. This day is not mine to conquer, control, and manipulate. This day is a pure gift; it comes as a limited blessing from God.

The day doesn't belong to me, and I can't seize it to make it mine. Sure, I will have plenty of opportunities to exercise personal agency. I will speak and move. I will interact with others. I will make thousands of decisions. I will triumph. I will fail. But to think that I have any claims of ownership on this day or any other is foolish and silly. There exists a spiritual arrogance and misdirection whenever I try to take for myself what belongs to God.

Life—all of it, including this day—comes as a gift with

which we are entrusted. For just a short while, we are blessed with the opportunity to live. How will I respond to God's gift? Will I treasure or squander the gift? How about you—what choices will you make?

The sun shines brightly through the trees. From where I am, it appears to be only a tiny burning orb. But it is so powerfully bright that I can't look directly into the sun without it leaving a blotch on my vision. There is movement as the sun rises in the sky. Soon its warmth will make the morning chill disappear and dry up the blanket of dew.

When each day is received and acknowledged as a gift something extraordinary happens. I find within myself a movement and a rising. From entitlement to gratitude. From pride to humility. I transition to a place of spiritual receptivity where I am more open to God's presence. When this happens (which isn't always, I continue to be a work in progress), I am more likely to be generous with my words, thoughts, and actions.

When I approach the day as a gift, I am a better

caretaker and steward of life. I fear less and trust more. I seek to be kinder and more compassionate in my dealings with others. Again, please hear me—I am a work in progress. I don't always treasure and honor my days. But when I do, I notice that life is better and my relationships are more vibrant.

At the heart of Jesus's teaching in parables is the clear message that God's Kingdom is at hand. It is today. Whether we welcomed the arrival of the day as the sun rose over our deck this morning or we slept in, we are now living in God's realm and reality. What we do with this sacred gift matters for us, our families, our community, nation, and all of creation. Every action. Every thought. So, let's start this day with gratitude and an awareness of the giftedness of this moment, so that we might really live every day.

CONCLUSION
EMBRACING LIFE

The leaves on the large oak trees that border and shade my backyard have started to change to a golden yellow. Alongside them, the maples contribute a reddish splendor. Potted chrysanthemums fill up the space on the deck where once herbs and zinnias flourished. Autumn's colors surround us. It is a beauty in which to find delight.

With my morning coffee from my favorite mug in hand, I settle into the cushion on a deck chair. Looking at the yard in these first moments of daylight, I smile. It has been a long time—both metaphorical and literal—since the ground was lifeless and covered with snow. Spring shared its blessing of buds, blossoms, and growth. Summer followed with its warmth. A transformation happened and is still in progress. Numerous perennial plants are going through their annual cycles—like actors, they walk on and off stage on cue. Change is a process that is constant.

Through efforts of planting, watering, pruning, and cutting, Katie and I have participated in the transformation of the backyard. Our efforts have made a difference, and we can look at our work with a sense of pride and satisfaction. That being said, I say "participated" because we did not create a single piece of it. Creation is something much bigger than us. It is more powerful and cannot be tamed in spite of our efforts or delusions.

While taking a swig of my rich, black coffee, I look at the backyard and smile again. In this moment, there is a simple joy. I know that things won't stay the same forever. I know that fall will turn to winter. I know that growth is followed by decay. Life is followed by death. But at this moment...there is gratitude. There is also the invitation found in the parables to live life to the fullness as a gift—imperfections and all.

Jesus's parables—the entire Bible for that matter—are not some ancient, hokey incantations or spells that you can recite to make everything flawlessly work out. In real life, there is no guarantee or magic formulas—do this, believe this, and life will turn out perfectly. Life just doesn't work that way. Those who hold such fantasy as their "truth" are ultimately disappointed.

They also miss the essence of scripture. The Bible is a love story between God and humanity. God chooses to be present in the midst of human life with all of its imperfections and messiness. Instead of avoiding struggle, pain, sorrow, mistakes, or unholiness, God enters with a passion and determination to remain. Here we find the wisdom and teaching of the cross. God, in the life of Jesus, endures the violence of a cross in solidarity with a broken and hurting humanity. The cross, with all its ugliness and hatred, rejection and failure, is the very place that God plants the seeds of resurrection.

The parables teach us that our life with God is less like a math problem and more like a dance step. Walk this way. Shuffle to the left, then to the right. The columns may not add up like you think they should or could, but that is alright. Don't overthink. Participating in God's Kingdom is so simple that a child could follow and yet so complicated that it takes a lifetime to master.

With my morning coffee in hand, I sit down on a deck chair and reflect. Beyond my smile and gratitude, I enter into the sacred space of a moment. By the grace of God, I am here. At this moment, at this time, I have the life God has given me. I breathe deeply in the present—not fully aware of where I've been or where I'm going, I push past and future to the side. For now, there is the present. It is a present for me to cherish and open. It is what I have, what I've been given. It is sufficient, sacred, and not to be squandered.

Settling into the comfortable cushion of the deck chair, I dwell in my identity as a child of God. God, through wisdom that passes my understanding, created my life (and yours too)! For that matter, all humanity has been chosen by God to bear the image, the essence, the "stuff" of God's being. Created in God's image, we are gifted. Our spirits remain connected to God's goodness and life—even though we may not "feel" it. Even though our brokenness may be all too real and undeniable—we remain connected to God's life.

I receive and embrace this truth: I am, you are, and we are part of God's life and Kingdom. As such, we have a worth that itself is sacred. We matter—no matter what anyone might tell us. No matter what we might say to ourselves, we matter and have a place in the universe that is unique. What is more, God invites us to engage, participate, dwell, and respond. For we are not alone; our backyard gardens are full of life. Look around and see the diverse plants and critters that inhabit the small portion of the world where we live.

The coffee in my cup will not last forever. As the dark liquid is depleted, I feel a restlessness begin to take over. A new day lies ahead of me. This present is begging me to open it and live into it. I have an opportunity to be who God created me to be—right now. I can choose to love, care, nurture, and be available to others.

Sure, I can run in the opposite direction. And I will, more often than I'd like to admit. I will lose my way, stumble, and stub my toe in the process. I'll need a healthy portion of forgiveness, kindness, compassion, and grace.

However, I find myself compelled, by the parables of Jesus, to make an effort. I will try, once again, to follow and be a faithful disciple. After all, the Kingdom of God is near. It is time to turn in God's direction.

Time to receive and embrace this moment that surrounds us. Time to breath and exhale. Time to choose the life that Jesus models.

Time to enter this day with gratitude. Time to love as God loves. Time to leave the comfort zone of the deck chair and live into the coming day.

Appendix A

You can use this book as a devotional during the season of Lent. Start on the First Sunday of Lent and follow the schedule below. During the time from Ash Wednesday to the first Sunday, read the Introduction material.

First Week in Lent -

Sunday -The Space Out Back and Within

Monday -The Parable of the Coffee Mug

Tuesday -The Parable of the Snow-Covered Tarp

Wednesday -The Parable of the Dried Hydrangea

Thursday -The Parable of the Shovel on the Back Porch

Friday -The Parable of the Frozen Ground

Saturday -Transforming the Yard: Winter's Sleep

Second Week in Lent

Sunday -Soil

Monday -The Parable of the Mud

Tuesday -The Parable of the Jackhammer

Wednesday -The Parable of the Compost Bin

Thursday -The Parable of the Dirty Hands

Friday -The Parable of the Considerate Neighbor

Saturday -Transforming the Yard: Digging into the Dirt

Third Week in Lent

Sunday -Seeds

Monday -The Parable of the Dandelion

Tuesday -The Parable of the Squash Blossom

Wednesday -The Parable of the Rhubarb

Thursday -The Parable of the Acorn

Friday -The Parable of the Surprise Seeds

Saturday -Transforming the Yard: Seeding the Beds

Fourth Week in Lent

Sunday -Light

Monday -The Parable of the Fire Table

Tuesday -The Parable of the Grill

Wednesday -The Parable of the Fireflies

Thursday -The Parable of the Solar Lights

Fifth Week in Lent

Holy Week

Holy Saturday -Transforming the Yard: Wonder and Gratitude

Easter - Conclusion

Appendix B

Daily Online Component

With the purchase of this book, you receive free access for you and a friend to the online component. Sign up using the link below. You will be asked to enter the code (all lower case). Once you register, you will receive the book's content through a series of daily emails sent automatically to your inbox in time for your morning coffee. In all, there are 40 days.

WEBSITE:
Lightfromthishill.com/backyard-parables-book

CODE: (lower case)
backyard

Please note: if you have ANY difficulty in accessing the page, please contact *Light From This Hill* at Lightfromthishill.com.

Notes: Where Do I Experience the Presence of God?

Notes: What ordinary things remind me of God's love?

Notes: What can I do today to reflect the light of Christ?

ABOUT THE AUTHOR

Ordained in 1997 as a pastor in the Evangelical Lutheran Church in America, The Rev. Dr. Walt Lichtenberger has served two congregations: Faith Lutheran Church in New Providence, New Jersey and St. James Lutheran Church in Burnsville, Minnesota.

In addition to over two decades of parish experience, he holds three advanced theological degrees. In 1997, he graduated from the Lutheran Theological Seminary in Gettysburg with a Masters of Divinity. This was followed in 2006, with a Masters of Sacred Theology from the Lutheran Theological Seminary in Philadelphia. In 2012, Walt graduated from Union Presbyterian Seminary in Richmond, Virginia with a Doctor of Ministry.

Walt lives with his wife and two sons in Savage, Minnesota.

Walt maintains a website filled with devotional materials that he has written. *Light From This Hill* is dedicated to shining a little light on your path. If you are interested in finding out more visit: www.lightfromthishill.com.

Made in the USA
Monee, IL
20 July 2021